Why Can't Read Maps

...and won't stop talking

Lessons men need to know about women

Allan & Barbara Pease

PEASE TRAINING INTERNATIONAL

First published by Pease Training International Pty. Ltd.
P.O. Box 12, Mona Vale. N.S.W. 2103. Australia.
Tel. (02) 99799000 Fax 99799099
Email peasetraining@compuserve.com
Web   www.peasetraining.com

National Library of Australia
Pease, Allan & Barbara
Why women can't read maps & won't stop talking
Communication (Psychology) 158'2
ISBN 0 9593 6586 9

Edited by The Peases, the Goldrings, Daniel Le Roux,
Diana Ritchie, Lisa Tierney and Penny Walters
Illustrations by John Hepworth
Concept by Barbara Pease
Cover Design by Luke Causby
Printed by Australian Print Group
Layout by Karen Stirling

Distributed by:
Australia and New Zealand: HarperCollins
United Kingdom: Orion Publishing
South Africa: Oxford University Press
SE Asia: Times Books

~ Introduction ~

Men and women are different. Not better or worse - but different.

Our objective in producing this mini-book is to help you, the reader, learn more about both yourself and the opposite sex so that your interaction and relationships can be more fulfilling, enjoyable and satisfying. It's full of commonsense advice and scientific facts that are both powerful and humorous.

We dedicate it to all the men and women who have ever sat up at 2am pulling their hair out as they plead with their partners, "But why don't you understand?" Relationships fail because men still don't understand why a woman can't be more like a man, and women expect their men to behave just like women do.

Enjoy!

Allan & Barbara Pease

~ Women's Emotions ~

"Yes Isobel ... I know it's a
mentally-deranged, sadistic axe-murderer ...
but it might be a mentally-deranged,
sadistic axe-murderer in need of help!!"

Admit mistakes.
A man won't admit
mistakes because he
thinks she won't love him.
But the reality is, a woman
will love him more.

When you're dealing with
an upset woman don't offer
solutions or invalidate her
feelings – just show her
you're listening.

Don't become angry when she gives you advice. For her, offering advice builds trust in a relationship and is not seen as a sign of weakness.

Talking about her problems is how a woman gets relief from stress. But she wants you to listen, not offer solutions.

Tell her about your problems.
For a woman, sharing
problems is a sign of trust
and friendship.

Ray plays his wedding video backwards. He says it's so he can see himself walk out of church, a free man.

A woman loves to receive a card from you. Buy an empty card and get another woman to teach you how to write a great message.

Acknowledge a woman's presence. When a man firegazes at the end of the day, it's easy for a woman to start feeling unloved.

How much you earn is not important. Women leave men, not because they are unhappy with what he can provide, but because they are emotionally unfulfilled.

Marriage has its good side.
It teaches you loyalty,
forbearance, tolerance, self-
restraint and other valuable
qualities you wouldn't need
if you'd stayed single.

A woman knows everything about her children. Men are vaguely aware of some short people also living in the house.

Women love to be touched.
A woman's skin is over ten
times more sensitive to touch
and pressure than a man's.
Use lots of appropriate
touching, but avoid groping.

In personality tests, men over-whelmingly choose adjectives for themselves including bold, competitive, capable, dominant, assertive, admired and practical. From the same list women choose warm, loving, generous, sympathetic, attractive, friendly and giving.

Under pressure, women talk
without thinking while men
act without thinking.

Women see admitting mistakes as a form of bonding and building trust. The last man to admit he'd made a mistake, however, was General Custer.

Be a woman's friend. When
she's upset she talks
emotionally to her friends.
An upset man would
rather rebuild a motor or
fix a leaking tap.

Be attentive if she's edgy.
Under stress or pressure, a
woman sees spending time
talking with her man as a
reward. She wants to talk and
cuddle. Men see talking as an
interference to the
problem-solving process and
prefer to fire-gaze.

Uptight men drink alcohol and
invade another country.
Uptight women eat chocolate
and invade shopping centres.

~ Female Brain Function ~

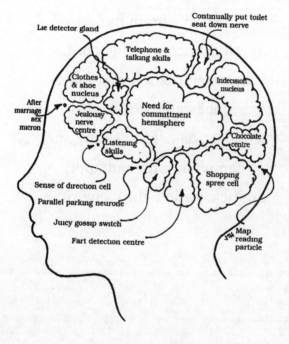

The Female Brain

A woman's brain has a 10% thicker connecting cord between the left and right lobes and 30% more connections. That's why she can walk, talk and apply lipstick – all at the same time.

Allow women to choose your clothing. One in every eight men is colour blind to blue, red or green and their brains have limited ability to match patterns and designs. That's why it's easy to spot a single man.

Buy fluffy toys for baby girls and ceiling mobiles for baby boys. Girls' brains are wired to respond to people and faces but boys' brains respond to objects and their shapes.

Girls mature much earlier than boys. By age seventeen, most girls can function as adults, while the boys are still pulling each other's pants down, giving a deadleg and lighting farts.

A woman's brain is organised for multi-tasking. She can do several unrelated things at once. She can drive a car, listen to the radio, talk on a hands-free telephone and think about her next appointment. Men can only do one thing at a time.

Women don't miss much.
Scans of women's brains
show 90% activity during
a resting state.

In a room of fifty couples it takes the average woman less than ten minutes to analyse the relationship between each couple in the room. She can see who's who, what's what and how they're all feeling.

Women love to feel secure. In bed, take your natural position - closest to the bedroom door. This is the symbolic act of defending the cave entrance.

Women use rest rooms as social lounges and therapy rooms. Women who go to a rest room as strangers can come out best friends. Men use rest rooms for biological reasons. And no man has ever been heard to say, "Hey Frank, I'm going to the toilet - you wanna come with me?"

Allow girls to study with
the TV or radio on.
Their brains can handle it,
but a boy's cannot.

Women have a greater variety of cones in the retina of the eye and wider peripheral vision than men. Their brain software allows them to receive an arc of at least 45 degrees to each side. This is why women rarely get caught ogling other men.

Don't criticise a woman for telling you to turn right when she really meant left. Women have more difficulty telling their left from their right hand because most use both sides of their brain for this task.

Women have language centres in both brains. If a man is injured on the left side of the head, he stands a chance of becoming mute. If a woman is hit in the same place, she'll probably keep right on talking.

In a restaurant, sit with
your back to the wall, facing
the restaurant entrance.
This makes you feel
comfortable and alert which
makes women feel secure.

Women add up aloud.
They usually work out
mathematical problems in the
left side of the brain, which
makes them slower at
calculus and is why they
perform mathematical
functions verbally.

On long trips, men should drive at night and women should drive during the day. Men's eyes see better into the distance at night than womens' and men can tell which side of the road the oncoming traffic is on.

Most women can brush their
teeth while walking and
talking on several topics. They
can make up and down strokes
with the toothbrush and, at
the same time, polish a mirror
using a circular movement
with the other hand. Most
men find this difficult, if not
impossible to do.

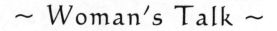

~ Woman's Talk ~

What Females Say ~ What Males Hear

For women, speech has a clear
purpose: to build relationships
and make friends – not to
solve problems. Let them talk.

When a woman talks at the end of the day, she doesn't want interruptions with solutions to her problems. You are not expected to respond, just to listen.

For men, not talking much
is perfectly natural. If women
spend time together and
don't talk, it would be
indicative of a major problem.

To get on better with women, talk more. If a man is with a group of women, his lack of talk makes the women think he is distant, sulky or doesn't want to join in.

Talking about day-to-day problems is how modern women cope with stress. They see it as bonding and being supportive.

A woman is four to six times more likely to touch another person in a social conversation than a man would. Don't misread a friendly touch.

It only seems like women are
talking over the top of you.
It's because women can speak
and listen simultaneously.
Their speech centres and
hearing funtions work at
the same time.

"Once I didn't talk to my
wife for six months," said
the husband. "I didn't
want to interrupt."

"I hope I haven't talked too much!!"

A woman talks to show
participation and build
relationships. If a woman is
talking to you a lot, she likes
you. If she's not talking to
you, you're in trouble.

If a woman wants to punish you she won't talk. Men call this 'the silent treatment'. The threat from a woman of, "I'll never talk to you again!" is one to be taken seriously.

When a woman talks, she sometimes hints at what she wants or beats around the bush. This is called 'indirect speech' and it builds relationships and rapport with others by avoiding aggression and confrontation.

If a woman sounds like she has a problem, ask, "Do you want me to listen as a man or a woman?" If she says she wants you to be a woman, just listen and encourage her.
If she wants you to be a man, you can offer solutions.

When she argues, she'll use
words that she doesn't really
mean, so don't take them
literally or try to define them.

A woman will think out loud. She sees it as being friendly and sharing. A man thinks she's giving him a list of problems that she expects him to fix and is likely to become anxious, upset or try to tell her what to do. Just listen.

Males use only three tones of
voice when speaking,
compared to a woman's five
tones. That's why men often
can't follow womens'
conversations and women
say, "Don't use that tone
of voice with me!"
when arguing.

Language does not have a specific location in male brains. Ask a teenage girl about the party she attended and she'll give you an articulate recitation of everything that happened – who said what to whom, how everyone felt and what they were wearing. Ask a teenage boy about the same party and he'll mumble, "Uhh…good."

A woman speaks a daily average of more than 20,000 communication 'words' to relate her message. This includes spoken words, voice changes and body language. A man's daily average adds up to around 7,000 — just over a third of the output of a woman.

A woman's talk is
unstructured and several
subjects can be discussed at
any one time with no
conclusions being reached.
Talking is like shopping.

For men, to talk is to relate the facts. They see the telephone as a communication tool for relaying facts and information to other people, but a woman sees it as a means of bonding.

~ Spatial Awareness ~

"Oh no! I Can't believe this, girls ...
look at this map! ... I think we were supposed to
turn right at that big green mountain..."

Don't ask geographically
challenged women to navigate.
Reading maps and
understanding where you
are relies on spatial ability.
Brain scans show that spatial
ability is strong in males
but poor in females. It's a
male hunting skill.

Around 90% of women have
limited spatial ability
compared to the average
man. That's why they have
so much trouble programming
a video player.

Most men can always point north - most women can't. Never give women directions like, "Head south" or "Go west for five kilometres". Instead, give directions involving landmarks such as "Drive past McDonald's and head for the building with the National Bank sign on top."

Never insist she parks the car
if she doesn't want to.
Estimating the distance
between the car bumper and
the garage wall while moving
is a spatial skill and is not
strong in most women.

Women can make excellent drag car racers because it's driving in a straight line. The winner is the person who has the fastest reaction time to the green light – an advantage that women have over men.

Overall, women have safer
driving records then men.

If local councils were made up
completely of women, reverse
and parallel parking would
no longer be allowed.

Women don't use rear-vision
mirrors. Their brains
use line-of-sight to
manoeuvre a vehicle.

Reflect a woman's expressions when you listen. A listening woman can use an average of six expressions in a ten-second period to mirror the emotions being expressed by the speaker.

Women drivers are less likely than a man to be hit from the side in an accident. Her greater peripheral vision allows her to see traffic approaching from the side. She is more likely to hit the front or back while attempting to reverse park.

To avoid arguments, don't ask a woman to read a map. If you don't have a specific area in the brain for map rotation, you turn it in your hands. It makes perfect sense to a woman to face a map in the direction she is travelling.

~ Women's Perception ~

Woman - the walking radar detector

When a woman tries on a new dress and asks, "How does it look?" don't give a simple response like "good." Respond the same way a woman would, by giving details. In other words, don't tell her what - tell her why. And do it in detail.

What is commonly called
'women's intuition' is mostly a
woman's acute ability to
notice small details and
changes in the appearance or
behaviour of others.

Share the remote control with
the woman in your life.

When a man completely shuts off, he's gone into problem solving mode. If a woman shuts off, there's trouble brewing and it's time for deep discussions.

Regularly take her out to dine.
Women see it as a way to
build and nurture a
relationship, discuss problems
or support a friend. Men see
eating out as a logical
approach to food – no cooking,
shopping or cleaning up.

If a woman is unhappy in
her relationships, she can't
concentrate on her work.
If a man is unhappy at
work, he can't focus on
his relationships.

If a woman asks you to choose between a pair of blue or gold shoes, don't do it. If you choose, you'll always be wrong. Ask her which she has chosen and give her confirmation why this is an excellent choice.

An architectural plan
of a house is seen two-
dimensionally by a female
brain, but male brains can
see it three dimensionally,
because their brains are
organised to see depth. Men
can see how a plan drawing
would look as a finished house.
Always show a woman a
three-dimensional version.

The most valuable thing
you can do is to listen to
a woman using listening
sounds and gestures, and
not offer solutions.

A woman reads the meaning of what is being said through voice intonation and the speaker's body language. This is exactly what you need to do to capture and keep her attention.

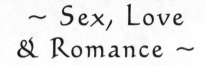

~ Sex, Love & Romance ~

"...I want openness, honesty and a
monogamous relationship. I'm not
into men who want to play games!"

Women don't like it when
you refer to sex as 'sex.'
Call it 'making love.'

How to Satisfy a Woman Every Time:
Caress, praise, pamper, relish, savour,
massage, fix things, empathise, serenade,
compliment, support, feed, soothe,
tantalise, humour, placate, stimulate,
stroke, console, hug, ignore fat bits,
cuddle, excite, pacify, protect, phone,
anticipate, smooch, nuzzle, forgive,
accessorise, entertain, charm, carry for,
oblige, fascinate, attend to, trust, defend,
clothe, brag about, sanctify, acknowledge,
spoil, embrace, die for, dream of, tease,
gratify, squeeze, indulge, idolise, worship.

How to Satisfy a Man Every Time:
Arrive Naked.

If a woman has an affair and says
it didn't mean anything, she's
probably lying. For a woman, sex
and love are intertwined.
One equals the other. That's
why women leave men who
have a casual fling.

Buy chocolates and champagne. Brown chocolate contains phenylethylamine that stimulates the love centre in a woman's brain. Champagne increases testosterone levels.

What's the difference between
a woman with PMT and a
terrorist? You can negotiate
with a terrorist.

People in love have been
shown to have better health
and are much less likely
to contract an illness than
those who are not.

Sex is the price women pay
for marriage. Marriage is
the price men pay for sex.

Women's Top 5 Turn-Ons

1. Romance
2. Commitment
3. Communications
4. Intimacy
5. Non-Sexual Touching

Monogamy turns women on.
A sexual liaison with another
woman is seen as the ultimate
betrayal and good reason to
finish a relationship.

Women recognise when
love doesn't exist. That's
why 80% of relationships
are ended by women.

The person who said that the
way to a man's heart is
through his stomach was
aiming too high.

Sex is great for your health.
Having an amorous interlude
an average of three times
every week burns up
35,000 kilojoules, which
is equal to running 130
kilometres in a year.

Feed her. Providing a woman with food stirs up primal female feelings.

A woman wants lots of sex
with the man she loves.
A man wants lots of sex.

Men give their penis a name because they don't want a stranger making 99% of their decisions for them.

A woman doesn't want sex for the same reasons a man does. A woman enters a new relationship looking for romance and love. Sex comes as a consequence.

When it comes to sex,
women need a reason;
men need a place.

Don't rush sex. Women's sex
drive is like an electric oven –
it heats slowly to its top
temperature and takes a long
time to cool down.

Of the hundreds of
popularised aphrodisiacs
around, none have been
scientifically shown to work.

Be understanding when
women have PMT. Women
suffering from PMT are four
to five times more likely to be
involved in a vehicle accident
if they are the driver.
Girls with PMT score
14% worse in mathematical
exams than non-sufferers.

"Let me get this straight Mrs Goodwin.
You say you're suffering PMT, you warned
your husband that unless he stopped flicking
channels on the remote control you'd blow
his brains out ... How did he respond?"

What's the difference between erotic and kinky? Erotic is when you use a feather. Kinky is when you use the whole chicken.

Tell her she's important to
you. For a woman to feel the
desire for sex, she needs to feel
loved, adored and significant.

When a man decides to
sensually touch a woman, he
does the things he prefers –
he gropes her boobs and
crotch. This is at the top of
most women's hate list.

Men don't fake orgasm – no
man wants to pull a face like
that on purpose.

Research shows that a
woman's orgasm rate is two
to three times higher in a
monogamous relationship
and four to five times higher
in a marital bed.

Making love is what a
woman does while a man
is bonking her.

Learn to dance. Women
love men who dance.
Dancing evolved to allow
close male/female contact
as a lead-up to courtship.

When a man sees a woman naked he becomes stimulated and aroused. When a woman sees a man naked, she usually bursts into laughter.

Only buy emotion-linked gifts
like flowers and a card.
Avoid practical things like
a toaster or carjack.

Most women prefer sex with the lights out – they can't bear to see a man enjoying himself.

Bring her flowers.
When they die, you can go
and get some more.

Why did they send so
many women with PMT
to the Gulf War? They
fought like animals and
retained water for four days.

Light a fire. Men have done
this for women for thousands
of years and it appeals to a
woman's romantic side.

It's great to be a man because
you can buy cucumbers and
marrows without getting
embarrassed and eat a
banana in front of builders.